The Regenerative Workplace:

A Pocket Guide to Lasting Corporate Wellness

CONTENTS

INTRODUCTION 1

CHAPTER 1 4

The Regenerative Wellness Framework Foundations for a Thriving Workforce

CHAPTER 2 11

Designing a Wellness-Driven Culture of Operational Excellence

CHAPTER 3 18

Leadership as Wellness Champions – Building a Culture of Support

CHAPTER 4 24

Customising Wellness for Diverse and Intergenerational Workforces

CHAPTER 5 31

Financial Resilience and Regenerative Financial Wellness

CHAPTER 6 38

Environmental Stewardship – Linking Wellness with Sustainability

CHAPTER 7 .... **46**

Future-Proofing Wellness with Resilience and Crisis Preparedness

CHAPTER 8 .... **54**

Innovation and Technology in Wellness

CHAPTER 9 .... **62**

Cultivating Community and Social Wellness Through Corporate Citizenship

CHAPTER 10 .... **69**

Measuring Wellness Impact and Building a Legacy of Health

CHAPTER 11 .... **77**

Lifelong Learning and Wellness – Fostering Continuous Growth

CHAPTER 12 .... **84**

Global Perspectives and Future Trends in Corporate Wellness

CONCLUSION **91**

Achieving Lasting Corporate Wellness – A Regenerative Vision for the Future

INTRODUCTION

The Regenerative Workplace

Workplace wellness has come a long way. Once considered a perk or an afterthought, it is now recognised as a cornerstone of sustainable success. But as organisations face increasing demands ranging from technological disruptions to global crises traditional approaches to wellness are no longer enough. To thrive in today's changing world, businesses need a new mindset: one that goes beyond sustainability to embrace regeneration.

The Regenerative Workplace is about creating systems, cultures, and environments where wellness not only sustains but grows and evolves over time. It's about empowering employees to be their healthiest, most productive selves while aligning wellness initiatives with long-term organizational goals.

This pocket guide is designed to provide you with actionable tools and strategies to build a regenerative workplace that supports your people, your business, and the world around you. Whether you're a leader, an HR professional, or simply someone passionate about wellness, this book offers insights to help you create lasting impact.

What Does Regenerative Wellness Mean?

Regenerative wellness focuses on enhancement rather than maintenance. Instead of merely preventing burnout or addressing immediate challenges, it prioritises long-term growth and adaptability. This approach recognises that wellness is multi-dimensional, encompassing:

- **Physical Health**: Promoting fitness, nutrition, and recovery.
- **Mental Health**: Building resilience and fostering emotional well-being.
- **Financial Health**: Supporting financial literacy and reducing stress.
- **Social Connections**: Cultivating a sense of belonging and purpose.
- **Environmental Impact**: Creating sustainable workplaces that benefit both employees and the planet.

Introduction

In a regenerative workplace, wellness becomes more than an initiative—it becomes a way of doing business.

Why This Book Matters Now

The past few years have highlighted the fragility of traditional systems. Global health crises, economic uncertainty, and rapid technological change have reshaped the way we work. Employees are looking for more than just a paycheck they're seeking balance, purpose, and support.

Organisations that fail to meet these needs risk losing talent, productivity, and relevance. Conversely, those that prioritise regenerative wellness can unlock innovation, improve employee retention, and build resilience for the future.

This book is your guide to making that shift. It's a practical, no-nonsense resource packed with frameworks, tips, and case studies to help you implement regenerative wellness in your organisation no matter its size or industry.

What You'll Learn

Throughout this book, you'll discover how to:

- **Audit and Enhance Your Workplace**: Identify areas where wellness can be improved and implement targeted strategies.
- **Build a Culture of Support**: Empower leaders and teams to champion wellness initiatives.
- **Leverage Technology and Innovation**: Use tools like AI, wearables, and dashboards to personalize and track wellness outcomes.
- **Align Wellness with Sustainability**: Create green initiatives that benefit employees and the environment.
- **Prepare for the Future**: Develop resilience plans to handle crises and ensure long-term success.

Each chapter offers actionable steps, real-world examples, and practical tools you can start using immediately.

Who This Book Is For

Whether you're leading a team, managing HR initiatives, or simply trying to improve workplace culture, this book is designed for you. It's a pocket guide, meant to be read, referenced, and revisited as you implement changes in your organisation.

A Call to Action

Creating a regenerative workplace isn't just about ticking boxes it's about fostering environments where people and organisations can truly thrive. As you read through this guide, I encourage you to take one actionable step at a time. Start small if needed, but start.

Your journey to lasting corporate wellness begins here. Together, let's build workplaces that sustain, innovate, and inspire for generations to come.

CHAPTER 1

The Regenerative Wellness Framework Foundations for a Thriving Workforce

Moving Beyond Traditional Wellness

In today's post-COVID business landscape, the rules of engagement have changed, and employees now expect much more from their employers. A common frustration I have is the misconception among business owners and corporations that corporate wellness simply means offering free gym memberships, a bowl of fruit on Fridays, access to Headspace, lunchtime yoga classes, or an Employee Assistance Program (EAP). While these are well-intentioned, they fail to address the deeper, systemic needs of both employees and organisations.

Traditional wellness programs that focus solely on managing symptoms of burnout, stress, or disengagement are no longer sufficient. What's truly needed is a proactive and regenerative approach one that doesn't just aim to maintain well-being but actively enhances it for both the organisation and its people.

A regenerative wellness framework is about creating a workplace ecosystem where health, resilience, and engagement flourish, where every aspect of well-being is interconnected and nurtured. It's a comprehensive model designed to foster thriving employees and organisations, enabling long-term success in an ever-changing world.

The Six Pillars of Regenerative Wellness

The regenerative wellness framework is built around six interconnected pillars, each addressing a critical dimension of well-being. Together, these pillars form the foundation for a thriving workforce and a resilient organisation.

1. Physical Wellness

- **Definition**: Physical wellness encompasses the health and vitality of the body, ensuring that employees have the energy and capacity to perform at their best.
- **Focus Areas**:
    - Nutrition and hydration
    - Fitness and movement
    - Sleep and recovery
- **Key Practices**:
    - Provide ergonomic workspaces that minimise physical strain.
    - Encourage active lifestyles through workplace fitness challenges, subsidised gym memberships, or standing desks.
    - Offer education on nutrition and sleep hygiene.

2. Mental Wellness

- **Definition**: Mental wellness involves fostering cognitive clarity, focus, and resilience. It ensures employees have the tools to manage stress and maintain productivity.
- **Focus Areas**:
    - Stress management
    - Focus and mindfulness
    - Cognitive agility
- **Key Practices**:
    - Incorporate mindfulness programs, meditation apps, or quiet spaces in the office.
    - Train managers to recognise and reduce stressors in the workplace.

Chapter 1

- Promote realistic workloads to prevent burnout.

3. Emotional Wellness

- **Definition**: Emotional wellness is the ability to recognise, understand, and manage emotions constructively. It also includes fostering a culture of empathy and emotional intelligence.
- **Focus Areas**:
    - Emotional resilience
    - Empathy and interpersonal relationships
    - Gratitude and positivity
- **Key Practices**:
    - Host workshops on emotional intelligence and conflict resolution.
    - Create channels for open communication where employees feel safe expressing concerns.
    - Celebrate achievements and foster a culture of gratitude.

4. Financial Wellness

- **Definition**: Financial wellness ensures employees feel secure about their financial future, reducing stress and fostering long-term stability.
- **Focus Areas**:
    - Financial literacy
    - Retirement planning
    - Emergency savings
- **Key Practices**:

- Provide access to financial advisors or online financial planning tools.
- Offer education on debt management, budgeting, and investing.
- Design compensation packages that reflect fair pay and promote financial equity.

5. Social Wellness

- **Definition**: Social wellness centres on the quality of relationships within the workplace and the broader community. It promotes a sense of belonging and collaboration.
- **Focus Areas**:
    - Team dynamics
    - Community engagement
    - Social purpose
- **Key Practices**:
    - Facilitate team-building activities that strengthen bonds among colleagues.
    - Partner with local organisations for volunteer opportunities.
    - Foster inclusivity and equity to ensure all employees feel valued.

6. Environmental Wellness

- **Definition**: Environmental wellness recognises the impact of the physical and ecological environment on well-being. A healthy environment nurtures productivity and sustainability.
- **Focus Areas**:
    - Eco-friendly workplace design

- Green initiatives and sustainability
- Connection to nature
- **Key Practices**:
  - Design workplaces with natural lighting, greenery, and improved air quality.
  - Reduce waste through recycling programs and sustainable procurement.
  - Promote active commuting options like biking or carpooling.

Interconnection of the Pillars

These six pillars don't exist in isolation. They are deeply interconnected, and progress in one area often supports others. For example:

- **Physical wellness** (e.g., better sleep) can enhance **mental clarity** and reduce stress.
- A strong sense of **social wellness** and belonging can improve **emotional resilience**.
- Addressing **financial wellness** reduces stress, supporting both **mental** and **physical wellness**.

By focusing on these interdependencies, organisations can create a multiplier effect, amplifying the overall impact of their wellness initiatives.

Why Regenerative Wellness Matters

The benefits of embracing a regenerative wellness framework are profound:

1. **Enhanced Employee Engagement**: Employees who feel supported in all aspects of their well-being are more engaged and committed to their work.
2. **Increased Productivity**: A healthy, focused, and energised workforce performs better, driving organisational success.

3. **Reduced Turnover and Absenteeism**: Employees are less likely to leave or take time off when their needs are met holistically.
4. **Resilience Against Crises**: Organisations with regenerative wellness cultures are better equipped to handle disruptions and adapt to change.

Leaders who prioritise regenerative wellness set their organisations apart as forward-thinking, adaptive, and resilient in the face of future challenges.

Actionable Step: Conduct a Wellness Audit

The first step toward implementing the regenerative wellness framework is to assess your organisation's current wellness landscape. A **wellness audit** evaluates strengths, challenges, and opportunities across the six pillars.

How to Conduct a Wellness Audit:

1. **Survey Employees**: Use anonymous surveys to gather feedback on their physical, mental, emotional, financial, social, and environmental wellness needs.
2. **Analyse Workplace Data**: Review data on absenteeism, turnover, and engagement to identify wellness trends and pain points.
3. **Benchmark Against Industry Standards**: Compare your wellness programs with those of leading organisations in your sector.
4. **Create a Wellness Report**: Summarise findings, highlight priority areas, and establish clear goals for improvement.

Real-World Example: Patagonia

Patagonia, the outdoor apparel company, exemplifies the power of regenerative wellness. The company's comprehensive wellness programs include on-site childcare, generous parental leave, and environmental sustainability initiatives. Patagonia's commitment to employee well-being and purpose-driven culture has earned it a reputation as one of the most admired companies globally. Employees report higher levels of engagement and purpose, directly contributing to Patagonia's long-term success.

Chapter 1

Conclusion: Laying the Foundation

The regenerative wellness framework is not a quick fix—it's a systemic, sustainable approach to creating a thriving organisation. By focusing on the six pillars and recognising their interconnectedness, leaders can create workplaces that don't just sustain well-being but actively enhance it.

In the chapters ahead, we'll explore how to embed these principles into your organisation's culture, processes, and strategy, creating a lasting legacy of wellness and resilience.

Action Step Recap: Begin with a wellness audit. Identify gaps and opportunities in your current approach and use these insights as the foundation for implementing regenerative wellness initiatives.

This chapter provides the foundation for the book, introducing the regenerative wellness framework and its practical applications, setting the stage for deeper exploration in subsequent chapters.

CHAPTER 2

Designing a Wellness-Driven Culture of Operational Excellence

Introduction: Wellness as a Strategic Asset

Wellness isn't a standalone initiative—it's a strategic asset that can drive efficiency, engagement, and long-term growth. A wellness-driven culture integrates well-being into the daily fabric of operations, making it a core organisational value rather than an optional add-on. By aligning wellness initiatives with operational excellence frameworks like Kaizen, Lean, and Six Sigma, companies can create sustainable processes that optimise both employee performance and organisational outcomes.

This chapter explores how to build a culture of operational excellence centred around wellness, leveraging continuous improvement methodologies and workplace design principles to foster health, productivity, and innovation.

The Case for Wellness-Driven Operational Excellence

Operational excellence is about creating systems and processes that deliver value efficiently and consistently. When wellness is embedded into these systems, organisations benefit from:

1. **Higher Employee Engagement**: Healthy, engaged employees are more productive and committed to their work.

2. **Reduced Waste**: Addressing burnout, absenteeism, and inefficiency through wellness reduces costs and operational friction.

3. **Continuous Improvement**: Wellness programs that evolve with employee needs align with the principles of adaptability and growth, ensuring sustained performance.

When wellness is treated as an integral part of operational strategy, it drives not only personal well-being but also organisational success.

Chapter 2

Leveraging Operational Excellence Frameworks for Wellness

1. Kaizen: Continuous Improvement in Wellness

- **Definition**: Kaizen, a Japanese term meaning "change for the better," focuses on continuous, incremental improvements.
- **Application to Wellness**:
    - Regularly gather employee feedback on wellness programs to identify opportunities for improvement.
    - Empower teams to propose wellness initiatives that address their specific needs, such as flexible schedules, fitness challenges, or mental health resources.
    - Conduct quarterly wellness reviews to track progress and refine strategies.
- **Example**: Toyota uses Kaizen principles to support employee wellness by continuously improving ergonomic workspaces and providing regular health check-ins.

2. Lean: Eliminating Waste in Wellness Processes

- **Definition**: Lean methodology emphasises maximising value while minimising waste.
- **Application to Wellness**:
    - Streamline wellness initiatives to focus on programs that deliver measurable impact. Eliminate redundant or underutilised initiatives.
    - Use data to identify inefficiencies, such as under-enrolled workshops or programs with low engagement and reallocate resources to more effective solutions.
    - Automate administrative tasks related to wellness, like scheduling health checkups or tracking participation, to reduce overhead.

- **Example**: A manufacturing company eliminated underused wellness perks and reinvested the savings into employee-requested mental health workshops, resulting in higher participation and satisfaction.

3. Six Sigma: Measuring and Optimising Wellness Performance

- **Definition**: Six Sigma uses data-driven methodologies to identify and eliminate defects, ensuring consistent quality.
- **Application to Wellness**:
    - Establish KPIs to measure wellness program success, such as participation rates, health outcomes, and employee satisfaction.
    - Use employee health data (anonymised) to identify patterns and tailor wellness initiatives accordingly.
    - Apply Six Sigma's DMAIC (Define, Measure, Analyse, Improve, Control) framework to systematically improve wellness outcomes.
- **Example**: A tech company used Six Sigma principles to analyse why their wellness programs had low engagement. By surveying employees, they discovered a lack of scheduling flexibility and redesigned programs to fit diverse work schedules.

Wellness-Centred Workplace Design

The physical environment plays a critical role in supporting employee wellness. A thoughtfully designed workplace can enhance both physical and mental health, leading to higher engagement and productivity.

1. Biophilic Design

- **Definition**: Biophilic design incorporates natural elements like greenery, natural light, and outdoor spaces into the workplace.
- **Benefits**:
    - Reduces stress and enhances creativity.

- Improves air quality and overall physical well-being.
- **Actionable Tips:**
  - Add indoor plants and natural light sources to workspaces.
  - Create outdoor break areas where employees can recharge.

2. Ergonomic Enhancements

- **Definition:** Ergonomic design ensures workspaces are comfortable, safe, and conducive to physical health.
- **Benefits:**
  - Reduces the risk of repetitive strain injuries and fatigue.
  - Enhances focus and productivity.
- **Actionable Tips:**
  - Provide adjustable desks and chairs that promote good posture.
  - Offer tools like keyboard wrist supports or anti-fatigue mats for employees in standing roles.

3. Quiet sones and Wellness Spaces

- **Definition:** Dedicated spaces for relaxation, meditation, or focused work.
- **Benefits:**
  - Supports mental clarity and stress reduction.
- **Actionable Tips:**
  - Create wellness rooms equipped with calming elements like soft lighting, comfortable seating, and mindfulness resources.

- Ensure quiet sones are free from distractions and accessible to all employees.

Embedding Wellness into Daily Operations

A wellness-driven culture doesn't rely solely on standalone programs; it integrates well-being into daily operations, ensuring it becomes a natural part of how work gets done.

1. Wellness-Infused Meetings

- **What to Do:**
    - Incorporate short wellness activities into meetings, such as breathing exercises or gratitude sharing.
    - Keep meetings concise and schedule breaks to avoid cognitive fatigue.
- **Example:** A marketing agency starts weekly team meetings with a two-minute mindfulness exercise, boosting focus and morale.

2. Flexible Work Policies

- **What to Do:**
    - Offer options like remote work, flexible hours, or compressed workweeks to support work-life balance.
    - Monitor outcomes to ensure flexibility doesn't compromise productivity.
- **Example:** A company with flexible hours saw a 20% increase in employee satisfaction and a 15% drop in absenteeism.

3. Encouraging Movement

- **What to Do:**
    - Promote active breaks during the workday, such as stretching sessions or walking meetings.

- Provide incentives for physical activity, such as fitness challenges with prises.
- **Example:** A healthcare organisation offers pedometers and rewards employees for meeting daily step goals, creating a culture of movement and camaraderie.

Actionable Step: Integrate Continuous Improvement into Wellness

To embed wellness into your culture of operational excellence, start with a **Continuous Improvement Cycle** for wellness initiatives:

1. **Plan**: Identify key wellness objectives, such as reducing stress or increasing physical activity.
2. **Do**: Implement targeted programs, such as ergonomic upgrades or mindfulness workshops.
3. **Check**: Measure outcomes using KPIs like participation rates, employee feedback, and health metrics.
4. **Act**: Refine initiatives based on feedback and results, ensuring they remain relevant and effective.

Real-World Example: Unilever

Unilever, a global consumer goods company, exemplifies the power of aligning wellness with operational excellence. The company integrates wellness into its core business strategy through initiatives like flexible work arrangements, mental health training for managers, and sustainable workplace design. Unilever's approach has resulted in lower absenteeism, higher engagement, and improved employee retention, proving that wellness-driven culture is a competitive advantage.

Conclusion: Operational Excellence Starts with Wellness

Designing a wellness-driven culture of operational excellence requires more than implementing individual programs—it's about embedding wellness into the very processes and systems that define your organisation. By leveraging frameworks like Kaizen, Lean, and Six Sigma, and creating wellness-friendly environments, leaders can build workplaces where health, efficiency, and innovation thrive together.

Action Step Recap: Identify one operational framework—Kaizen, Lean, or Six Sigma—that resonates with your organisation. Apply it to a specific wellness initiative, such as improving participation in fitness programs or streamlining mental health resources. Measure the results, refine your approach, and watch as wellness becomes a driver of operational excellence.

This chapter combines strategic insights and practical applications, giving leaders the tools to make wellness a core component of their operational success.

CHAPTER 3

Leadership as Wellness Champions – Building a Culture of Support

Introduction: The Role of Leaders in Driving Wellness

Great organisations are built by great leaders, and in the modern workplace, a leader's role extends beyond driving results—they must champion wellness as a fundamental component of success. When leaders model wellness and actively support their teams, they create an environment where employees feel valued, supported, and empowered to perform at their best.

This chapter focuses on how leaders can act as catalysts for wellness. We'll explore the mindset, skills, and strategies leaders need to foster a wellness-driven culture and provide actionable steps to equip them for this crucial role.

Why Leadership Matters in Wellness

Leadership sets the tone for an organisation. A wellness program can only succeed when leaders actively engage with and model the **principles of well-being themselves.** Employees are more likely to embrace wellness initiatives when they see their leaders practicing and promoting them authentically.

Key Impacts of Leadership on Wellness

1. **Building Trust and Engagement**: Leaders who prioritise employee wellness create a sense of trust, showing their teams that they care about more than just results.
2. **Driving Cultural Change**: Leadership is the most influential factor in shaping workplace culture. Wellness-focused leaders inspire organisational change that aligns with well-being and purpose.

3. **Enhancing Team Resilience**: Leaders who model resilience and emotional intelligence help their teams navigate challenges and maintain high performance under pressure.

Developing the Wellness Champion Mindset

For leaders to be effective wellness champions, they must embrace a mindset that prioritises empathy, adaptability, and growth.

1. Empathy and Emotional Intelligence

- **Why It Matters**: Empathy enables leaders to connect with their teams on a personal level, understanding their needs and challenges.

- **Action Steps**:
    - Schedule regular one-on-one check-ins with team members to discuss not just work but overall well-being.
    - Practice active listening by focusing on what employees are saying without interruption or judgment.
    - Attend emotional intelligence workshops to enhance self-awareness and interpersonal skills.

2. Modelling Wellness Behaviours

- **Why It Matters**: Employees take cues from their leaders. When leaders practice wellness themselves, it encourages others to do the same.

- **Action Steps**:
    - Take breaks during the workday and encourage your team to do the same.
    - Participate in wellness initiatives like fitness challenges or mindfulness sessions to demonstrate commitment.
    - Share personal wellness goals or habits, such as a focus on sleep, exercise, or stress management.

3. Cultivating Resilience and Adaptability

- **Why It Matters:** Resilient leaders help their teams remain calm and focused during times of uncertainty.
- **Action Steps:**
    - Lead by example during crises by maintaining composure and focusing on solutions.
    - Offer resources for stress management and resilience training, such as meditation apps or professional development courses.
    - Celebrate small wins to build morale and keep teams motivated.

Training Leaders to Support Wellness

Leadership development programs should include specific training to help leaders understand and prioritise wellness. Here's how to build a wellness-focused leadership training initiative:

1. Core Training Topics

- **Wellness Awareness**: Educate leaders on the six pillars of wellness (physical, mental, emotional, financial, social, and environmental) and how they impact performance.
- **Mental Health First Aid**: Train leaders to recognise signs of stress, burnout, or mental health struggles and provide appropriate support or referrals.
- **Empathy and Communication Skills**: Teach leaders how to foster open, supportive conversations about wellness without judgment.

2. Practical Exercises for Leaders

- **Role-Playing Scenarios**: Practice responding to wellness-related challenges, such as an employee experiencing burnout or struggling with work-life balance.

- **Wellness Action Plans**: Encourage leaders to create personal wellness action plans, outlining how they will support their own well-being and that of their team.

3. Ongoing Development and Feedback

- Provide regular feedback to leaders on how well they are supporting wellness in their teams.
- Offer advanced workshops or certifications in areas like resilience coaching, DEI-focused wellness, or crisis management.

Building a Culture of Support

Beyond individual actions, leaders must foster a culture of wellness throughout their teams and the broader organisation.

1. Normalise Conversations About Wellness

- **Why It Matters**: Removing the stigma around discussing wellness helps employees feel safe seeking support.
- **Action Steps**:
    - Begin team meetings with check-ins, asking how everyone is feeling or what support they may need.
    - Share wellness resources openly, such as mental health hotlines or employee assistance programs.

2. Encourage Peer Support

- **Why It Matters**: Peer relationships can be a powerful source of encouragement and accountability in wellness efforts.
- **Action Steps**:
    - Create peer mentorship programs where employees can support each other in areas like financial wellness or fitness goals.

- Celebrate team wellness achievements, such as completing a group fitness challenge or reducing stress levels during a busy period.

3. Align Wellness with Organisational Values

- **Why It Matters**: Integrating wellness into the organisation's mission ensures it becomes a lasting priority.
- **Action Steps**:
    - Include wellness goals in team objectives and performance reviews.
    - Recognise and reward leaders who excel in fostering a wellness-driven culture.

Real-World Example: Google's Leadership in Wellness

Google has long been recognised as a leader in employee wellness. Its managers are trained to prioritise employee well-being, with a focus on mental health, work-life balance, and career development. Initiatives like mindfulness programs and flexible work policies are directly supported by leadership, creating a culture where wellness is ingrained in every aspect of the workplace. Google's commitment to wellness has resulted in high employee engagement and retention, proving the power of leadership in driving well-being.

Actionable Step: Create a Leadership Training Program for Wellness

Here's a step-by-step guide to develop a wellness-focused leadership training program:

1. **Assess Current Leadership Gaps**: Survey employees to identify areas where leadership support for wellness can improve.
2. **Design Training Modules**: Include topics like mental health awareness, resilience coaching, and empathetic leadership.
3. **Implement Workshops**: Host in-person or virtual workshops to train leaders in wellness practices.

4. **Monitor Progress**: Use feedback and performance metrics to evaluate the impact of the training program and make adjustments as needed.

Conclusion: Leaders as Catalysts for Wellness

Leaders are the driving force behind any successful wellness initiative. By modelling wellness behaviours, fostering empathy, and prioritising team support, leaders can transform workplace culture into one that thrives on well-being. When leaders champion wellness, it becomes a shared value that permeates every level of the organisation.

Action Step Recap: Start by training leaders to support wellness. Develop a program that includes empathy building, mental health awareness, and practical wellness strategies. Encourage leaders to model these practices, and watch as your organisation transforms into a healthier, more engaged workplace.

This chapter lays out a clear, actionable pathway for empowering leaders to become wellness champions, ensuring that well-being is integrated into both culture and operations.

CHAPTER 4

Customising Wellness for Diverse and Intergenerational Workforces

Introduction: The Challenge of Diversity in Workplace Wellness

In today's workplace, diversity isn't just a goal—it's a reality. Modern organisations are more diverse than ever, encompassing multiple generations, cultural backgrounds, and personal identities. While diversity brings richness and innovation, it also creates unique challenges for designing wellness programs that resonate across such a broad spectrum of needs.

A "one-size-fits-all" approach to wellness simply won't work. For wellness programs to succeed, they must be adaptable, inclusive, and responsive to the diverse needs of employees. This chapter explores how to customise wellness initiatives to support a diverse and intergenerational workforce, ensuring that every employee feels valued and included.

Understanding Workforce Diversity

1. Generational Diversity

- **Overview**: Most workplaces today are multigenerational, with Baby Boomers, Generation X, Millennials, and Generation s working side by side.
- **Key Challenges**:
    - Different generations have unique wellness priorities. For example:
        - Baby Boomers may focus on physical health and retirement planning.

- Millennials may prioritise mental health and work-life balance.
- Gen s may value flexibility and purpose-driven wellness initiatives.
- Communication styles and technology preferences vary across generations, affecting engagement with wellness programs.

2. Cultural and Ethnic Diversity

- **Overview**: Employees from different cultural backgrounds bring unique perspectives on wellness, influenced by traditions, values, and societal norms.
- **Key Challenges**:
  - Cultural stigmas may affect attitudes toward mental health or certain types of wellness initiatives.
  - Dietary preferences or restrictions may vary, affecting nutrition-focused programs.

3. Diversity in Gender and Identity

- **Overview**: Employees' gender identities, sexual orientations, and personal identities can influence how they experience and engage with wellness programs.
- **Key Challenges**:
  - Gender-specific health concerns, such as maternity care or men's mental health, may require tailored support.
  - LGBTQ+ employees may face unique stressors, such as discrimination or lack of inclusion in certain wellness activities.

Chapter 4

Designing Inclusive Wellness Programs

Inclusive wellness programs address the diverse needs of employees while fostering a sense of belonging and respect. Here's how to make wellness initiatives adaptable and equitable:

1. Tailor Programs to Generational Needs

- **What to Do:**
    - Conduct generational surveys to understand wellness priorities for each group.
    - Offer a mix of initiatives to cater to different preferences, such as tech-enabled solutions for younger employees and in-person activities for older generations.
- **Examples:**
    - Provide ergonomic solutions and physical health screenings for Baby Boomers.
    - Create mindfulness and stress management programs tailored to Millennials.
    - Offer financial literacy workshops that appeal to Gen s's focus on early financial planning.

2. Incorporate Cultural Sensitivity

- **What to Do:**
    - Consider cultural practices and values when designing wellness programs.
    - Provide options that accommodate dietary restrictions, religious observances, or cultural preferences.
- **Examples:**
    - Offer diverse food choices at wellness events to cater to a variety of cultural diets.

- Respect cultural holidays and provide flexible schedules for observances.

3. Address Gender-Specific Wellness Needs

- **What to Do:**
  - Include programs that address specific health concerns, such as maternity care, menopause support, or prostate health awareness.
  - Ensure wellness initiatives are inclusive of all gender identities and sexual orientations.
- **Examples:**
  - Host workshops on parenting and childcare support for all genders.
  - Partner with organisations that provide LGBTQ+-specific mental health resources.

Integrating DEI Principles into Wellness

Diversity, Equity, and Inclusion (DEI) are essential for building wellness programs that resonate with all employees. Here's how to weave DEI into your wellness strategy:

1. Foster Equitable Access

- **Why It Matters**: Not all employees have the same access to resources, whether due to location, job roles, or personal circumstances.
- **Action Steps**:
  - Ensure wellness programs are available to remote, part-time, and frontline employees.
  - Provide flexible participation options, such as virtual sessions or asynchronous learning tools.

2. Promote Psychological Safety

- **Why It Matters**: Employees need to feel safe expressing their wellness needs without fear of judgment or bias.
- **Action Steps**:
    - Train leaders to create inclusive spaces where wellness discussions are normalised.
    - Offer anonymous feedback channels for employees to share their thoughts on wellness programs.

3. Celebrate Diversity in Wellness

- **Why It Matters**: Highlighting the diversity of wellness experiences fosters a sense of belonging and respect.
- **Action Steps**:
    - Host cultural wellness days, celebrating practices like yoga, tai chi, or traditional nutrition from different cultures.
    - Share stories of diverse employees and their wellness journeys, showcasing the unique ways people approach well-being.

Using Technology to Personalise Wellness

Technology can help bridge the gap between diverse wellness needs, providing personalised solutions that cater to individual preferences and circumstances.

1. Wellness Platforms and Apps

- Use digital platforms that offer a range of wellness options, from fitness challenges to mental health resources.
- Leverage AI-driven tools that personalise recommendations based on individual employee data, such as preferred activities or health goals.

2. Wearable Technology

- Offer wearable devices, such as fitness trackers, to monitor physical health and encourage active lifestyles.
- Use aggregated, anonymised data to identify trends and refine wellness programs.

3. Virtual Wellness Resources

- Provide virtual access to wellness workshops, counselling sessions, and fitness classes to accommodate remote and global teams.
- Use multilingual platforms to make resources accessible to employees in different regions.

Actionable Step: Create a Wellness Persona Map

To design inclusive wellness programs, start by creating a **Wellness Persona Map**:

1. **Identify Employee Segments**: Divide your workforce into key groups based on factors like generation, cultural background, and job roles.
2. **Map Their Wellness Needs**: Gather feedback through surveys, focus groups, or interviews to understand what each group values in wellness.
3. **Design Targeted Solutions**: Use the insights to develop wellness programs tailored to each persona, ensuring broad relevance and appeal.

Real-World Example: PwC's Inclusive Wellness Strategy

Professional services firm PwC has developed wellness initiatives that reflect its commitment to diversity and inclusion. Their programs include:

- **Mental Health First Aid Training**: Leaders are trained to recognise and address mental health concerns across diverse teams.

- **Flexible Work Options**: Employees can choose schedules that fit their lifestyles, accommodating various cultural and generational needs.
- **Diversity-Specific Resources**: PwC offers LGBTQ+-inclusive mental health support and mentorship programs for women leaders.

These initiatives have led to higher employee satisfaction and engagement, demonstrating the power of inclusive wellness.

Conclusion: Embracing Diversity for Stronger Wellness Outcomes

Customising wellness for diverse and intergenerational workforces is not just a nice-to-have—it's a business imperative. By understanding the unique needs of your employees and designing programs that celebrate and respect their differences, you create a workplace where everyone can thrive.

Action Step Recap:

1. Conduct a diversity-focused wellness survey to identify the unique needs of your workforce.
2. Develop a Wellness Persona Map to guide program design.
3. Launch initiatives that cater to generational, cultural, and gender-specific needs, ensuring inclusivity at every level.

A truly inclusive wellness program isn't just about meeting needs—it's about making every employee feel valued, respected, and empowered. As you embrace this approach, you'll foster a culture of belonging that drives engagement, performance, and innovation.

This chapter combines strategic insights, practical tools, and real-world examples to help leaders design wellness programs that honour and celebrate diversity.

CHAPTER 5

Financial Resilience and Regenerative Financial Wellness

Introduction: The Overlooked Pillar of Wellness

When we think about wellness, physical and mental health often come to mind first. Yet financial wellness is one of the most significant factors influencing overall well-being. Financial stress doesn't just impact employees' personal lives; it affects productivity, engagement, and decision-making at work.

In today's economy, many employees—regardless of income level—struggle with financial insecurity. Whether it's debt, insufficient savings, or uncertainty about retirement, financial stress is a major driver of anxiety and burnout. Organisations that prioritise financial wellness empower employees to manage their finances with confidence, reducing stress and enhancing resilience.

This chapter explores the key components of regenerative financial wellness and provides actionable strategies for integrating financial well-being into your workplace.

The Importance of Financial Wellness in the Workplace

1. The Hidden Cost of Financial Stress

- Financial stress affects workplace performance in several ways:
    - **Decreased Productivity**: Employees distracted by financial concerns are less focused and effective.
    - **Higher Absenteeism**: Financially stressed employees are more likely to take time off due to mental health or personal issues.

- **Turnover and Retention**: Employees who feel unsupported in their financial well-being may leave for organisations offering better benefits.

2. Financial Resilience as a Strategic Advantage

- Financial resilience is the ability to adapt and thrive in the face of economic challenges, whether personal or organisational.
- By supporting financial wellness, companies can build a workforce that is more focused, engaged, and capable of weathering uncertainties.

The Components of Regenerative Financial Wellness

1. Financial Literacy

- **Definition**: Providing employees with the knowledge and skills to make informed financial decisions.
- **Key Focus Areas**:
    - Budgeting and saving
    - Debt management
    - Understanding credit scores
- **Actionable Steps**:
    - Host financial literacy workshops or webinars on topics like saving for emergencies, investing, and managing debt effectively. - Provide access to online resources or tools that simplify financial planning, such as budgeting apps or calculators. - Partner with financial advisors to offer one-on-one consultations for employees seeking personalised guidance.

2. Emergency Savings Programs

- **Definition**: Helping employees build a financial cushion for unexpected expenses.

- **Key Focus Areas**:
    - Encouraging small, consistent savings habits.
    - Offering employer-matched contributions to emergency savings accounts.
- **Actionable Steps**:
    - Set up automatic savings programs where employees can allocate a percentage of their pay check to a dedicated savings account.
    - Provide education on the importance of emergency savings and how it can reduce financial stress.
    - Collaborate with financial institutions to create easy-to-use, low-fee savings solutions tailored for employees.

3. Retirement Planning and Long-Term Security

- **Definition**: Ensuring employees are prepared for their financial future beyond their working years.
- **Key Focus Areas**:
    - Educating employees on retirement planning options.
    - Offering retirement savings programs with employer contributions.
- **Actionable Steps**:
    - Provide access to retirement planning tools and seminars to help employees understand 401(k) plans, IRAs, and investment options.
    - Offer regular financial wellness checkups where employees can track their progress toward long-term financial goals.
    - Highlight the benefits of starting early and the power of compound interest through engaging, easy-to-understand presentations.

4. Debt Management Support

- **Definition**: Assisting employees in managing and reducing debt burdens to improve financial stability.

- **Key Focus Areas**:
    - Credit card and loan repayment strategies.
    - Managing student loans effectively.

- **Actionable Steps**:
    - Partner with financial wellness providers to offer debt counselling services.
    - Introduce student loan repayment benefits, such as matching payments or refinancing options.
    - Provide workshops on strategies to prioritise and eliminate high-interest debt.

5. Financial Equity and Pay Transparency

- **Definition**: Ensuring employees are compensated fairly and have equal access to financial resources.

- **Key Focus Areas**:
    - Conducting pay equity audits to address disparities.
    - Offering transparent compensation structures.

- **Actionable Steps**:
    - Regularly review pay scales and ensure alignment with market standards and internal equity.
    - Publish clear guidelines on how salary decisions are made and offer opportunities for employees to discuss compensation concerns.

- Offer financial literacy programs targeted to groups who may face systemic financial disadvantages, such as women or underrepresented minorities.

Integrating Financial Wellness into Organisational Culture

1. Embedding Financial Wellness in Benefits Packages

- **Why It Matters**: Financial wellness benefits signal that the organisation values its employees' holistic well-being.
- **Actionable Steps**:
    - Incorporate financial planning resources into existing wellness programs.
    - Offer flexible benefits that allow employees to choose the financial resources that suit their individual needs, such as student loan support, childcare subsidies, or eldercare benefits.

2. Encouraging Open Conversations About Money

- **Why It Matters**: Financial concerns are often stigmatised, making it harder for employees to seek help.
- **Actionable Steps**:
    - Normalise discussions about financial well-being in team meetings or through company-wide communication.
    - Create safe spaces, such as anonymous surveys or confidential counselling services, for employees to share concerns.

3. Aligning Financial Wellness with Organisational Purpose

- **Why It Matters**: When financial wellness aligns with a company's values, it becomes a natural extension of its mission.

- **Actionable Steps**:
    - Include financial wellness goals in your corporate social responsibility (CSR) initiatives.
    - Partner with local organisations or nonprofits to provide financial education resources to employees and their communities.

Real-World Example: Starbucks' Financial Wellness Programs

Starbucks has set a benchmark in financial wellness with its innovative programs, such as:

1. **College Achievement Plan**: Offering full tuition coverage for eligible employees pursuing degrees through Arizona State University, reducing the financial burden of higher education.
2. **Bean Stock Program**: Allowing employees to share in the company's success through stock options, promoting financial empowerment and long-term wealth building.
3. **Comprehensive Benefits**: Including financial literacy resources and tools to help employees plan for retirement and manage debt.

These initiatives have significantly boosted employee engagement and retention while fostering a culture of financial security and opportunity.

Measuring the Impact of Financial Wellness

To ensure the success of your financial wellness programs, it's essential to track their effectiveness. Here are key metrics to monitor:

1. **Participation Rates**: Track the percentage of employees using financial wellness resources, such as workshops, savings programs, or retirement plans.
2. **Employee Satisfaction**: Use surveys to gauge how employees feel about their financial security and the resources provided.

3. **Productivity Metrics**: Monitor changes in absenteeism, presenteeism, and overall productivity to assess the impact of reduced financial stress.
4. **Turnover Rates**: Evaluate whether employees are staying longer due to improved financial benefits and support.

Actionable Step: Launch a Financial Wellness Initiative

Here's a step-by-step guide to creating a financial wellness program:

1. **Assess Employee Needs**: Conduct anonymous surveys or focus groups to identify the most pressing financial concerns.
2. **Design Tailored Programs**: Offer a mix of resources, such as savings tools, debt counselling, and retirement planning, to address diverse needs.
3. **Promote Engagement**: Use multiple communication channels to educate employees about available resources and encourage participation.
4. **Measure Outcomes**: Track key metrics and gather employee feedback to refine the program over time.

Conclusion: Building Financial Resilience for a Thriving Workforce

Financial wellness isn't just about helping employees manage money—it's about fostering a culture of security, empowerment, and resilience. When organisations invest in regenerative financial wellness, they create a ripple effect that benefits both individuals and the company as a whole.

Action Step Recap: Start by implementing one financial wellness initiative—such as offering financial literacy workshops or launching an emergency savings program. Measure its impact, refine the approach, and expand over time.

By making financial wellness a cornerstone of your organisational strategy, you'll not only reduce stress and boost engagement but also position your company as a leader in holistic employee well-being.

This chapter equips leaders with practical tools and strategies to prioritise financial wellness, making it an integral part of their organisation's wellness culture.

CHAPTER 6

Environmental Stewardship – Linking Wellness with Sustainability

Introduction: The Connection Between Wellness and the Environment

The health of the environment directly impacts human wellness. From the air we breathe to the spaces we occupy, the ecological context of our lives plays a vital role in our physical, mental, and emotional well-being. As organisations strive to create workplaces that support employee wellness, they must also consider how their environmental practices contribute to or detract from that goal.

Environmental stewardship is not only a responsibility but also an opportunity to align wellness initiatives with sustainability goals. By integrating eco-friendly practices into the workplace, companies can enhance employee health, reduce their ecological footprint, and create a culture of responsibility and purpose.

This chapter explores how organisations can connect wellness and sustainability to foster both individual and planetary well-being.

Why Environmental Stewardship Matters for Wellness

1. Physical Health Benefits

- Cleaner air, access to natural light, and reduced exposure to pollutants directly improve physical health outcomes.
- Eco-friendly office designs reduce sick building syndrome, allergies, and respiratory issues.

2. Mental and Emotional Well-Being

- Access to green spaces and natural environments is proven to lower stress, improve focus, and enhance mood.

- Employees feel a greater sense of purpose when their organisation demonstrates commitment to environmental responsibility.

3. **Organisational Impact**

- Sustainable practices resonate with employees and customers, enhancing brand reputation and loyalty.
- Green initiatives reduce operational costs through energy efficiency, waste reduction, and sustainable resource management.

Integrating Environmental Stewardship into Workplace Wellness

1. Sustainable Workspace Design

- **What to Do:**
  - Use biophilic design principles to integrate natural elements like greenery, natural light, and water features into the office environment.
  - Optimise air quality with proper ventilation and air purification systems.
- **Action Steps:**
  - Add indoor plants to improve air quality and aesthetics.
  - Maximise access to natural light by arranging workstations near windows.
  - Use sustainable building materials and eco-friendly office furniture.

2. Green Energy and Resource Management

- **What to Do:**
  - Transition to renewable energy sources for office operations.

- Reduce energy consumption through smart technologies and employee engagement.
- **Action Steps**:
  - Install energy-efficient lighting and motion sensors to minimise waste.
  - Educate employees on energy-saving practices, such as unplugging devices and minimising paper use.
  - Invest in solar panels or partner with green energy providers to power facilities.

3. Sustainable Commuting Options

- **What to Do**:
  - Encourage employees to use eco-friendly commuting options, such as biking, carpooling, or public transportation.
  - Offer incentives for reducing carbon footprints during their daily commute.
- **Action Steps**:
  - Provide bike racks and shower facilities for employees who cycle to work.
  - Subsidise public transportation passes or implement carpool programs.
  - Host "active commuting challenges" to promote walking or biking.

4. Waste Reduction and Recycling

- **What to Do**:
  - Implement robust waste reduction and recycling programs.

- Encourage employees to adopt sustainable habits in their daily routines.

- **Action Steps**:
    - Provide clearly labelled recycling bins throughout the workplace.
    - Switch to reusable or biodegradable materials for office supplies, such as utensils, cups, and stationery.
    - Organise company-wide "zero waste" days to raise awareness and promote sustainability.

Engaging Employees in Environmental Wellness

Environmental stewardship thrives when employees feel personally connected to green initiatives. Here's how to engage your workforce in creating a more sustainable workplace:

1. Green Teams

- **What They Do**: Create employee-led teams that spearhead sustainability initiatives and engage colleagues in green practices.
- **Action Steps**:
    - Empower green teams to identify areas for improvement and propose eco-friendly solutions.
    - Provide budgets and resources to support their efforts, such as tree planting drives or energy audits.

2. Wellness Challenges with a Sustainability Focus

- **What They Do**: Combine wellness goals with sustainability, encouraging employees to adopt habits that benefit both their health and the environment.
- **Action Steps**:

- Host challenges like "commute green week" or "meatless Mondays" to promote eco-friendly behaviours.
- Offer rewards for employees who consistently participate in green initiatives, such as gift cards or extra time off.

3. Education and Awareness

- **What to Do:** Educate employees about the connection between wellness and sustainability.
- **Action Steps:**
    - Host workshops or lunch-and-learns on topics like reducing carbon footprints or sustainable living at home.
    - Share regular updates on the company's sustainability progress and achievements.

Connecting Environmental Stewardship to Community Impact

Environmental stewardship doesn't stop at the workplace. Companies can extend their impact by involving employees in community-focused sustainability efforts.

1. Corporate Social Responsibility (CSR) Programs

- **What to Do:** Partner with local organisations to support environmental causes, such as conservation, waste cleanup, or renewable energy projects.
- Action Steps:
- **Organise team volunteer days focused on community cleanups or tree planting**
- Partner with nonprofits to fund or participate in renewable energy or conservation initiatives.

- Incorporate CSR goals into annual wellness and sustainability reports to showcase the organisation's broader impact.

2. Employee Volunteer Programs

- **What to Do**: Encourage employees to participate in sustainability efforts outside the office by offering time and resources.
- **Action Steps**:
    - Provide paid volunteer days for employees to work on local environmental projects.
    - Host group events like beach cleanups, recycling drives, or community garden projects.
    - Match employee donations to environmental charities, doubling their impact.

3. Education and Advocacy in the Community

- **What to Do**: Extend your organisation's environmental expertise to the broader community.
- **Action Steps**:
    - Host community workshops or webinars on sustainable practices.
    - Partner with schools or community groups to educate future generations about the importance of environmental stewardship.
    - Share your company's success stories and strategies to inspire others to adopt eco-friendly practices.

Real-World Example: Patagonia's Environmental Stewardship

Patagonia is a prime example of a company integrating environmental wellness into its organisational DNA. They have set the gold standard with initiatives such as:

- **Sustainable Product Design**: Patagonia uses recycled materials in its products and offers repair services to extend their lifespan, reducing waste.
- **1% for the Planet Program**: The company donates 1% of its annual sales to environmental organisations.
- **Employee-Led Activism**: Patagonia encourages employees to participate in environmental campaigns and provides paid time off for volunteer activities. This alignment of wellness, sustainability, and community engagement has strengthened Patagonia's brand identity and deepened employee loyalty.

Measuring the Impact of Environmental Wellness Initiatives

To ensure your environmental wellness initiatives are effective, it's crucial to track their impact. Here are key metrics to monitor:

1. **Employee Engagement**: Measure participation rates in green initiatives and feedback from employees about their experiences.
2. **Environmental Metrics**: Track reductions in waste, energy use, and carbon emissions to quantify the environmental impact.
3. **Cost Savings**: Monitor cost reductions from energy efficiency programs, reduced resource consumption, and waste management improvements.
4. **Community Impact**: Evaluate the success of community partnerships and the number of participants in volunteer programs.

Actionable Step: Start a Green Initiative at Work

Here's how to get started with a simple yet impactful green initiative:

1. **Choose a Focus Area**: Identify a pressing environmental issue, such as energy efficiency, waste reduction, or sustainable commuting.
2. **Engage Employees**: Form a green team or hold a brainstorming session to gather ideas and gain buy-in.

3. **Set Clear Goals**: Define measurable objectives, such as reducing energy consumption by 20% or increasing recycling rates by 50%.
4. **Implement the Program**: Roll out the initiative with clear communication and ongoing support.
5. **Track Progress**: Regularly evaluate your program's success and refine it based on employee feedback and environmental data.

Conclusion: Aligning Wellness with Environmental Stewardship

Environmental stewardship isn't just about saving the planet—it's about creating a healthier, more inspiring workplace where employees thrive. By linking wellness initiatives with sustainability goals, organisations can enhance employee well-being while driving meaningful impact at a global scale.

Action Step Recap: Start by assessing your organisation's current environmental practices. Then, implement one eco-friendly initiative—whether it's sustainable workspace design, a green commuting program, or a waste reduction effort. Engage your employees every step of the way and measure your progress to refine your strategy.

A workplace that prioritises environmental stewardship is more than just a place to work—it's a community united by purpose and a commitment to making a difference.

This chapter connects wellness with sustainability, offering actionable strategies and examples for embedding environmental stewardship into organisational culture.

CHAPTER 7

Future-Proofing Wellness with Resilience and Crisis Preparedness

Introduction: The Need for Resilience in an Uncertain World

In an increasingly unpredictable world, organisations must be prepared for challenges ranging from global pandemics to economic downturns, natural disasters, and technological disruptions. These crises can have a profound impact on employees' physical and mental well-being, often leading to burnout, anxiety, and disengagement.

The key to navigating these challenges lies in building resilience—both at the individual and organisational levels. Resilience is not just the ability to bounce back from adversity; it's about thriving in the face of uncertainty and emerging stronger. This chapter explores strategies for fostering resilience and implementing crisis preparedness plans that safeguard employee wellness and organisational stability.

What Is Resilience in the Workplace?

1. Individual Resilience

- **Definition**: The capacity of an employee to manage stress, adapt to change, and maintain well-being during difficult circumstances.
- **Key Traits**:
    - Emotional regulation
    - Optimism and problem-solving skills
    - Adaptability and perseverance

2. Organisational Resilience

- **Definition**: The ability of a company to anticipate, prepare for, respond to, and recover from disruptions while minimising harm to its people and operations.

- **Key Traits**:
    - Strong communication channels
    - Flexible and adaptive processes
    - A culture of trust and mutual support

Building Individual Resilience in Employees

1. Provide Resilience Training

- **What It Is**: Workshops and resources that equip employees with skills to manage stress, adapt to change, and develop a growth mindset.

- **Action Steps**:
    - Offer workshops on mindfulness, emotional intelligence, and stress management.
    - Use real-life scenarios and role-playing exercises to teach employees how to navigate challenges.
    - Provide access to resilience-building tools like apps, podcasts, or guided meditations.

2. Foster a Growth Mindset

- **What It Is**: Encouraging employees to view challenges as opportunities for learning and development.

- **Action Steps**:
    - Celebrate effort and progress, not just outcomes, to reinforce the value of persistence.

- Share stories of how teams or individuals overcame adversity and emerged stronger.
- Include growth mindset principles in performance reviews and feedback sessions.

3. Encourage Work-Life Balance

- **What It Is**: Ensuring employees have the time and energy to recharge outside of work.
- **Action Steps**:
  - Offer flexible working hours or remote work options to support personal needs.
  - Encourage employees to use vacation time and avoid overworking.
  - Provide wellness programs that address mental and physical health, such as fitness challenges or counselling services.

Creating a Resilient Organisational Culture

1. Develop Crisis-Ready Leadership

- **What It Is**: Training leaders to remain calm, decisive, and empathetic during crises.
- **Action Steps**:
  - Host leadership training programs focused on crisis management and communication skills.
  - Encourage leaders to practice transparency and honesty when addressing teams during challenging times.
  - Build a network of peer support among leaders to share best practices and resources.

2. Strengthen Communication Channels

- **What It Is**: Ensuring that employees have access to timely and accurate information during disruptions.

- **Action Steps**:
    - Establish clear protocols for internal communication during a crisis.
    - Use multiple platforms—emails, messaging apps, town halls—to reach all employees effectively.
    - Create a feedback loop where employees can share concerns and receive responses.

3. Build Trust and Psychological Safety

- **What It Is**: Creating an environment where employees feel safe expressing concerns and seeking help.

- **Action Steps**:
    - Train managers to recognise signs of stress or burnout and respond with empathy.
    - Regularly reinforce the availability of mental health resources and Employee Assistance Programs (EAPs).
    - Encourage open discussions about challenges without fear of judgment or repercussions.

Crisis Preparedness Plans for Employee Wellness

1. Mental Health Crisis Response Plan

- **Why It Matters**: Mental health crises can escalate quickly if not addressed effectively, impacting both individuals and teams.

- **Action Steps**:
    - Train managers in mental health first aid, equipping them to respond to emergencies compassionately.

- Partner with licensed counsellors or therapists to provide immediate support.
- Develop a clear escalation protocol for addressing serious concerns, such as suicidal ideation or severe anxiety.

2. Physical Health Preparedness

- **Why It Matters**: Physical health risks, such as pandemics or workplace injuries, can disrupt operations and endanger employees.
- **Action Steps**:
  - Establish protocols for managing health crises, including access to testing, vaccination, or emergency care.
  - Invest in workplace safety equipment and training programs to prevent accidents.
  - Provide sick leave policies that encourage employees to prioritise their health without fear of financial loss.

3. Remote Work Contingency Plan

- **Why It Matters**: The ability to pivot to remote work ensures continuity during disruptions like natural disasters or global pandemics.
- **Action Steps**:
  - Equip employees with the technology and tools they need to work effectively from home.
  - Develop clear guidelines for remote work expectations, collaboration, and communication.
  - Provide resources for ergonomic home office setups and mental health support for remote employees.

Engaging Employees in Resilience Initiatives

1. Resilience Challenges

- Organise team challenges focused on resilience-building activities, such as fitness goals, mindfulness practices, or stress reduction strategies.

2. Employee Feedback

- Regularly solicit feedback on wellness and resilience programs to identify gaps and areas for improvement.

3. Recognition and Rewards

- Celebrate employees who demonstrate resilience and adaptability, reinforcing these values across the organisation.

Real-World Example: Johnson & Johnson's Resilience Initiatives

Johnson & Johnson has embedded resilience into its workplace culture through:

1. **Energy for Performance Program**: A workshop that trains employees to manage energy levels, stress, and focus for peak performance.

2. **Global Mental Health Ambassadors**: Employees are trained to support colleagues and connect them to resources.

3. **Crisis Preparedness**: The company has robust protocols for supporting employees during emergencies, from health crises to natural disasters.

These efforts have resulted in higher employee engagement and a stronger organisational culture, proving the value of resilience-focused wellness strategies.

Measuring the Success of Resilience and Crisis Preparedness

To evaluate the impact of resilience initiatives, track the following metrics:

1. **Employee Stress Levels**: Use surveys or tools like pulse checks to assess changes in stress levels over time.
2. **Engagement and Retention**: Monitor whether employees feel more engaged and committed during challenging periods.
3. **Crisis Response Time**: Evaluate the efficiency and effectiveness of your crisis management protocols.

Actionable Step: Create a Resilience Playbook

Develop a **Resilience Playbook** for your organisation by:

1. Identifying key risks and challenges that could impact employee wellness.
2. Designing training programs and resources to address these challenges.
3. Creating clear, actionable plans for mental health crises, physical health risks, and operational disruptions.
4. Regularly updating the playbook based on employee feedback and lessons learned from past crises.

Conclusion: Building a Future-Ready Workplace

Resilience isn't about avoiding challenges—it's about facing them head-on with strength, adaptability, and purpose. By fostering individual resilience, creating a supportive culture, and preparing for crises, organisations can protect their most valuable asset: their people.

Action Step Recap:

1. Train employees and leaders in resilience-building techniques.
2. Establish mental health, physical health, and operational crisis response plans.
3. Regularly evaluate and refine your approach to ensure long-term success.

By prioritising resilience and preparedness, you're not just safeguarding wellness—you're future-proofing your organisation for whatever lies ahead.

This chapter offers a roadmap for embedding resilience into workplace culture and preparing for future challenges.

CHAPTER 8

Innovation and Technology in Wellness

Introduction: Technology as a Wellness Catalyst

The rapid advancement of technology is reshaping every aspect of our lives, including how we approach wellness in the workplace. From AI-driven health solutions to wearable devices, technology has the potential to transform wellness programs by making them more personalised, accessible, and effective. But innovation alone is not enough; it must be strategically integrated into a wellness framework that prioritises human needs.

This chapter explores the role of technology in wellness, highlighting how organisations can use cutting-edge tools to enhance employee well-being, while also addressing potential risks like over-reliance on data or privacy concerns.

The Benefits of Technology-Driven Wellness Programs

1. Personalisation

- Technology enables wellness programs to be tailored to individual employee needs and preferences.
- Examples:
    - AI algorithms that analyse health data to recommend personalised fitness or stress management plans.
    - Apps that adjust mental health resources based on user feedback.

2. Accessibility

- Digital platforms remove barriers to participation by making wellness resources available anytime, anywhere.

- Examples:
    - Virtual fitness classes accessible to remote employees.
    - Telehealth services for counselling or medical consultations.

3. Real-Time Feedback

- Wearable devices and wellness apps provide instant data on health metrics like heart rate, steps, or sleep patterns.
- Examples:
    - Fitness trackers that encourage movement throughout the day.
    - Stress monitoring apps that offer breathing exercises in response to elevated stress levels.

4. Data-Driven Insights

- Aggregated, anonymised data helps organisations identify wellness trends and refine their programs.
- Examples:
    - Identifying high levels of stress in specific departments and targeting interventions accordingly.
    - Measuring the effectiveness of wellness initiatives through participation and outcome data.

Integrating Technology into Your Wellness Strategy

1. AI and Predictive Analytics

- **What It Is**: Using AI to predict and address wellness needs based on employee data.

Chapter 8

- **Applications**:
    - Identifying early signs of burnout or declining health based on work patterns, survey results, or wearable data.
    - Offering personalised wellness recommendations tailored to each employee's goals.
- **Action Steps**:
    - Partner with vendors specialising in AI-driven wellness tools.
    - Ensure transparency about how data is collected and used to build employee trust.

2. Wearable Devices

- **What They Are:** Gadgets like fitness trackers, smartwatches, and stress monitors that collect health data.
- **Applications**:
    - Encouraging physical activity by tracking steps, calories, and exercise habits.
    - Monitoring stress levels and prompting relaxation techniques during high-stress periods.
- **Action Steps**:
    - Offer subsidies for employees to purchase wearable devices or provide them as part of the wellness program.
    - Host challenges or competitions that incentivise employees to use wearables for health goals.

3. Telehealth and Virtual Wellness Services

- **What They Are:** Online platforms that connect employees with healthcare providers, counsellors, or wellness coaches.

- **Applications**:
    - Providing mental health counselling through video calls or chat services.
    - Offering nutrition consultations or personalised fitness plans remotely.
- **Action Steps**:
    - Partner with telehealth providers to offer on-demand access to healthcare services.
    - Promote the use of virtual wellness platforms through onboarding and ongoing communications.

4. Wellness Apps and Portals

- **What They Are**: Digital platforms that consolidate wellness resources and track employee engagement.
- **Applications**:
    - Centralised access to wellness content, such as workout videos, mindfulness exercises, and financial planning tools.
    - Gamified wellness programs that reward healthy behaviours.
- **Action Steps**:
    - Evaluate wellness platforms based on employee needs and ease of use.
    - Regularly update content and features to keep employees engaged.

Chapter 8

Addressing Challenges in Technology-Driven Wellness

1. Data Privacy and Security

- **The Challenge**: Employees may be hesitant to share health data due to concerns about misuse or breaches.

- **Solutions**:
    - Clearly communicate how data will be used and ensure it remains anonymous and confidential.
    - Partner with vendors that prioritise robust security measures and compliance with privacy regulations (e.g., GDPR, HIPAA).

2. Over-Reliance on Technology

- **The Challenge**: While technology enhances wellness programs, it cannot replace human connection or empathy.

- **Solutions**:
    - Balance digital tools with in-person wellness initiatives, such as workshops or team activities.
    - Train managers to use technology as a supplement, not a replacement, for personal interactions with their teams.

3. Employee Engagement

- **The Challenge**: Technology adoption may be uneven, with some employees hesitant to use new tools.

- **Solutions**:
    - Provide training and support to ensure employees understand how to use wellness technology effectively.
    - Foster a culture of experimentation, encouraging employees to try different tools without fear of judgment.

Future Trends in Wellness Technology

1. Biofeedback Devices

- Wearables that measure real-time physiological responses, such as heart rate variability or skin conductivity, to track stress and relaxation levels.
- Future applications: Personalised meditation or breathing exercises based on biofeedback data.

2. Virtual Reality (VR) for Wellness

- Immersive VR environments for stress relief, guided meditation, or virtual fitness classes.
- Future applications: Team-building exercises or workplace simulations to enhance collaboration and reduce stress.

3. AI-Powered Chatbots

- Chatbots that provide instant wellness advice or emotional support.
- Future applications: Integrating chatbots into employee portals for seamless access to wellness resources.

4. Blockchain for Wellness Data

- Blockchain technology to enhance data security and give employees control over their wellness information.
- Future applications: Allowing employees to share specific data points with employers or healthcare providers without compromising privacy.

Actionable Step: Implement a Technology Pilot Program

To integrate technology into your wellness strategy, start with a pilot program:

1. **Assess Needs**: Survey employees to identify which wellness tools they find most valuable, such as wearables, apps, or telehealth services.
2. **Select Tools**: Partner with trusted vendors to test a small-scale implementation of chosen technologies.
3. **Engage Employees**: Provide training and incentives to encourage adoption and gather feedback throughout the pilot phase.
4. **Evaluate Results**: Analyse participation, satisfaction, and outcomes to determine whether the program should be scaled or refined.

Real-World Example: Accenture's Technology-Driven Wellness Programs

Accenture, a global consulting firm, has embraced technology to support employee wellness through initiatives like:

- **Accenture Mindful**: A digital platform offering guided mindfulness sessions, resilience training, and stress management resources.
- **Wearable Tech Integration**: Employees can participate in challenges using fitness trackers, fostering a culture of movement and health.
- **AI-Powered Insights**: The company uses analytics to identify trends in employee wellness and tailor programs accordingly.

These initiatives have improved employee engagement and overall well-being, demonstrating the potential of technology to transform workplace wellness.

Conclusion: Balancing Innovation with Human Connection

Technology offers powerful tools to enhance workplace wellness, but it's most effective when paired with a human-cantered approach. By leveraging AI, wearables, telehealth, and other innovations, organisations can create wellness programs that are personalised, accessible, and impactful.

Action Step Recap:

1. Start with a pilot program to test the effectiveness of wellness technologies.
2. Balance digital tools with in-person initiatives to maintain human connection.
3. Regularly evaluate and adapt your technology strategy to meet evolving employee needs.

By integrating technology thoughtfully, you can create a workplace that supports employees in achieving their wellness goals while embracing the future of innovation.

This chapter equips organisations with actionable strategies to leverage technology for wellness while addressing potential challenges.

CHAPTER 9

Cultivating Community and Social Wellness Through Corporate Citizenship

Introduction: The Role of Community in Wellness

Wellness is not just an individual endeavour—it thrives in communities. Strong social connections and a sense of belonging are essential for emotional resilience, mental health, and overall well-being. In the workplace, fostering social wellness means creating an environment where employees feel connected, supported, and purposeful.

Corporate citizenship—the practice of integrating social responsibility into business operations—plays a critical role in building these connections. By engaging in community-focused initiatives, organisations can cultivate social wellness both within and beyond their walls, enriching employee experiences and leaving a positive impact on society.

This chapter explores how to build social wellness through intentional community-building and corporate citizenship, with actionable strategies for creating a workplace culture that values connection and purpose.

The Importance of Social Wellness

1. Individual Impact

- Employees with strong social connections report higher levels of happiness, reduced stress, and better mental health.
- Social isolation or lack of community can lead to disengagement, burnout, and poor performance.

2. Organisational Impact

- Teams with strong bonds are more collaborative, innovative, and productive.

- A workplace culture of connection enhances employee retention and loyalty.

3. Societal Impact

- Organisations that contribute to their communities build trust, reputation, and goodwill, creating a positive cycle of impact that benefits everyone.

Strategies for Building Social Wellness Within the Workplace

1. Foster Team Collaboration and Connection

- **What to Do**:
    - Create opportunities for employees to collaborate meaningfully, both on work projects and social activities.
- **Action Steps**:
    - Host regular team-building activities that go beyond traditional icebreakers, focusing on shared experiences and collective problem-solving.
    - Create mentorship programs where employees can build relationships across departments or generations.
    - Encourage "buddy systems" for new hires to help them integrate socially.

2. Encourage Cross-Departmental Interaction

- **What to Do**:
    - Break down silos and create spaces for employees from different teams to connect.
- **Action Steps**:
    - Organise cross-functional brainstorming sessions or innovation workshops.

Chapter 9

- Create shared spaces, like lounges or cafeterias, that encourage informal interactions.
- Rotate team leads or project members periodically to foster new relationships.

3. Celebrate Milestones and Achievements

- **What to Do**:
    - Recognise and celebrate employee milestones, both professional and personal.
- **Action Steps**:
    - Celebrate birthdays, work anniversaries, and team achievements with meaningful gestures or small celebrations.
    - Use a shared platform or newsletter to highlight employee stories, successes, and contributions.

Corporate Citizenship and Community Engagement

1. Community Volunteering Programs

- **What They Are**: Initiatives that encourage employees to volunteer their time and skills to support local or global causes.
- **Action Steps**:
    - Organise volunteer days where teams work together on community projects, like cleaning up parks or serving at food banks.
    - Partner with local nonprofits to offer ongoing volunteer opportunities.
    - Provide paid volunteer leave to enable employees to contribute without sacrificing income.

2. Social Impact Projects

- **What They Are:** Programs that align the organisation's resources and expertise with broader societal goals.

- **Action Steps:**
  - Identify causes that align with your company's values, such as education, sustainability, or healthcare.
  - Allocate a portion of profits or resources to fund community projects, like building schools or supporting clean water initiatives.
  - Involve employees in the planning and execution of these projects to deepen their sense of purpose.

3. Employee-Led Initiatives

- **What They Are:** Programs that empower employees to spearhead social wellness and community projects.

- **Action Steps:**
  - Create a grant or funding program that allows employees to propose and lead social impact initiatives.
  - Establish a "Community Action Committee" where employees can organise and advocate for specific causes.
  - Recognise and reward employees who take leadership roles in community efforts.

Building Social Wellness Through Shared Purpose

1. Align Corporate Values with Community Goals

- **What to Do:**
  - Ensure your organisation's values and mission align with the causes it supports.

- **Action Steps**:
  - Conduct a values audit to identify overlaps between company goals and community needs.
  - Communicate the alignment clearly to employees, customers, and stakeholders.

2. Host Purpose-Driven Events

- **What to Do**:
  - Organise events that combine social wellness with a sense of shared purpose.
- **Action Steps**:
  - Host charity walks, runs, or fitness challenges that raise funds for causes.
  - Organise hackathons or innovation challenges where employees create solutions for community issues.

3. Strengthen Employee Purpose Through Storytelling

- **What to Do**:
  - Highlight the impact of your organisation's social and community initiatives.
- **Action Steps**:
  - Share stories of how company efforts have improved lives, whether through employee newsletters, videos, or social media.
  - Encourage employees to share their own experiences of participating in community initiatives.

Measuring the Impact of Social Wellness Initiatives

1. Employee Engagement

- Use surveys and feedback tools to measure how employees feel about their connections with colleagues and the broader community.

2. Volunteer Participation

- Track the number of employees involved in volunteer activities and the total hours contributed.

3. Community Impact

- Measure the outcomes of your social impact initiatives, such as funds raised, resources donated, or lives impacted.

4. Retention and Productivity Metrics

- Analyse whether employees involved in social wellness programs show higher retention rates, satisfaction, or productivity.

Real-World Example: Salesforce's Community Focus

Salesforce, a global leader in CRM solutions, exemplifies corporate citizenship through its **1-1-1 Model**:

- **1% of Equity**: Donated to philanthropic causes.
- **1% of Product**: Provided to nonprofits for free.
- **1% of Time**: Employees are encouraged to volunteer, with Salesforce offering seven paid days off for volunteering annually. This model has fostered a culture of connection, purpose, and social impact, with employees reporting higher levels of engagement and satisfaction.

Actionable Step: Launch a Social Wellness Initiative

Here's how to get started with a social wellness program:

1. **Identify a Cause**: Survey employees to find out which causes resonate most with your team.
2. **Create a Plan**: Partner with community organisations or charities to define specific initiatives, like volunteer days or fundraising events.
3. **Engage Employees**: Promote the initiative through internal communications and incentives, such as recognition or rewards.
4. **Measure and Share Impact**: Track participation and outcomes and celebrate successes with the team to reinforce the value of the program.

Conclusion: Creating a Culture of Connection and Purpose

Social wellness is about more than building relationships—it's about creating a sense of belonging and shared purpose. By fostering connection within the workplace and extending impact to the broader community, organisations can enhance employee well-being while driving meaningful societal change.

Action Step Recap:

1. Foster team and cross-departmental connections through intentional activities and programs.
2. Launch volunteer and social impact initiatives that align with your company's values.
3. Measure the impact of your efforts on employees and the community, and refine your approach based on feedback.

A workplace that prioritises social wellness and corporate citizenship becomes more than a place to work—it becomes a force for good, inspiring employees to thrive and make a difference.

This chapter emphasises the importance of social wellness and corporate citizenship, providing actionable strategies and real-world examples to create meaningful impact.

CHAPTER 10

Measuring Wellness Impact and Building a Legacy of Health

Introduction: The Importance of Measurement in Wellness Programs

In today's data-driven world, what gets measured gets managed—and wellness is no exception. While organisations increasingly invest in wellness initiatives, many struggle to demonstrate their tangible impact. Without clear metrics and reporting, wellness programs risk being undervalued, underfunded, or misaligned with organisational goals.

Measuring the effectiveness of wellness programs is not just about tracking ROI; it's about understanding their broader impact on employee well-being, organisational resilience, and long-term success. This chapter explores how to establish key performance indicators (KPIs), use data to refine wellness strategies, and create a lasting legacy of health.

Why Measuring Wellness Impact Matters

1. Accountability

- Demonstrating the impact of wellness programs ensures accountability to stakeholders, including employees, leadership, and investors.

2. Strategic Alignment

- Measuring results allows wellness initiatives to align more closely with business objectives, such as productivity, engagement, and retention.

3. Continuous Improvement

- Data-driven insights help refine wellness programs, ensuring they evolve with employee needs and industry trends.

4. Storytelling and Legacy

- Clear metrics and success stories make it easier to communicate the value of wellness programs, inspiring both internal and external audiences.

Establishing Wellness KPIs

1. Participation Metrics

- **What to Measure**: Track how many employees are engaging with wellness programs, such as fitness challenges, counselling sessions, or workshops.
- **Why It Matters**: High participation indicates that programs are relevant and accessible.
- **Examples**:
    - Percentage of employees enrolled in wellness programs.
    - Attendance rates for workshops or events.

2. Engagement Metrics

- **What to Measure**: Assess how actively employees participate and how committed they are to wellness initiatives.
- **Why It Matters**: Engagement reflects the perceived value and effectiveness of programs.
- **Examples**:
    - Frequency of app usage (e.g., wellness platforms or fitness trackers).
    - Repeat participation in wellness challenges.

3. Health Outcomes

- **What to Measure**: Evaluate changes in employees' physical, mental, and emotional health.
- **Why It Matters**: Positive health outcomes are the ultimate goal of any wellness program.
- **Examples**:
    - Reduction in sick days or absenteeism.
    - Improvements in self-reported stress levels or fitness scores.

4. Organisational Metrics

- **What to Measure**: Track the broader impact of wellness programs on business performance.
- **Why It Matters**: Demonstrating alignment with business goals helps secure leadership buy-in.
- **Examples**:
    - Employee retention rates.
    - Changes in productivity or team performance.
    - Cost savings from reduced healthcare claims.

5. Financial Metrics

- **What to Measure**: Assess the ROI of wellness initiatives by comparing costs to benefits.
- **Why It Matters**: Quantifying financial impact strengthens the case for continued investment.
- **Examples**:
    - Healthcare cost savings.
    - Revenue gains from improved productivity.

Chapter 10

Tools and Methods for Measuring Wellness Impact

1. Surveys and Feedback

- **What They Do**: Collect qualitative and quantitative data directly from employees about their wellness experiences.
- **Action Steps**:
    - Use anonymous surveys to gauge satisfaction, engagement, and perceived benefits.
    - Conduct focus groups or one-on-one interviews for deeper insights.

2. Wellness Dashboards

- **What They Are**: Digital platforms that aggregate and visualise wellness data in real time.
- **Action Steps**:
    - Partner with vendors to implement dashboards that track metrics like participation, engagement, and health outcomes.
    - Use dashboard insights to identify trends and refine programs.

3. Wearable Devices and Apps

- **What They Do**: Provide real-time health data, such as steps taken, calories burned, or stress levels.
- **Action Steps**:
    - Offer employees the option to integrate wearables or apps into wellness programs.
    - Aggregate anonymised data to assess collective health trends.

4. HR and Business Data

- **What It Does**: Leverage existing organisational data to measure the indirect impact of wellness.
- **Action Steps**:
    - Analyse absenteeism, turnover, and healthcare claims to identify wellness-related changes.
    - Integrate wellness metrics with broader HR dashboards to show holistic impact.

Refining Wellness Programs Based on Data

1. Identify Gaps

- **What to Do**: Use data to pinpoint areas where wellness programs are underperforming or missing key employee needs.
- **Examples**:
    - Low participation in physical fitness programs may indicate a need for more variety or flexibility.
    - High stress levels in specific departments may suggest targeted interventions.

2. Test and Iterate

- **What to Do**: Pilot new initiatives and use feedback to refine them before scaling.
- **Examples**:
    - Launch a mindfulness program for a small group and measure engagement before rolling it out company wide.
    - Use A/B testing to determine the most effective communication strategies for promoting wellness programs.

3. Share Success Stories

- **What to Do**: Highlight tangible outcomes to build momentum and inspire participation.

- **Examples**:
    - Share testimonials from employees who achieved personal health goals through wellness programs.
    - Use metrics to showcase the company-wide impact, such as improved productivity or reduced absenteeism.

Building a Legacy of Health

1. Create a Wellness Scorecard

- **What It Is**: A tool for tracking and communicating wellness performance over time.

- **Components**:
    - Key metrics (participation, engagement, health outcomes, ROI).
    - Year-over-year comparisons to show progress.
    - Qualitative highlights, such as employee testimonials or community impact stories.

2. Document Best Practices

- **What It Is**: A repository of lessons learned, successful strategies, and actionable insights.

- **Components**:
    - Case studies of successful wellness initiatives.
    - Guidelines for adapting programs to meet evolving needs.

- Recommendations for integrating wellness with organisational strategy.

3. Communicate Impact Externally

- **What to Do**: Share your organisation's wellness successes with stakeholders, customers, and the broader community.

- **Action Steps**:
  - Publish an annual wellness impact report highlighting achievements and goals.
  - Use social media and company blogs to showcase wellness milestones and employee stories.

Real-World Example: Deloitte's Holistic Approach to Wellness Metrics

Deloitte is known for its robust wellness measurement strategy, which includes:

1. **Participation Tracking**: Monitoring engagement in programs like fitness classes and mental health workshops.
2. **Employee Surveys**: Regularly assessing satisfaction and perceived benefits.
3. **Health Data Analysis**: Using aggregated data to track changes in stress levels, sleep quality, and physical activity.
4. **Business Impact Metrics**: Measuring improvements in productivity, retention, and healthcare cost savings.

Deloitte's focus on both qualitative and quantitative metrics ensures its wellness programs remain impactful and aligned with organisational goals.

Actionable Step: Develop a Wellness Measurement Plan

Here's how to get started:

1. **Define Objectives**: Identify the key outcomes you want to achieve, such as improved health or reduced absenteeism.

2. **Select Metrics**: Choose KPIs that align with your objectives and are measurable within your organisation.

3. **Implement Tools**: Use surveys, dashboards, or wearable devices to collect data.

4. **Analyse and Refine**: Regularly review metrics, identify trends, and adjust programs as needed.

5. **Communicate Results**: Share insights with leadership, employees, and other stakeholders to build support and drive engagement.

Conclusion: Measuring Impact for Lasting Change

Measuring the impact of wellness programs is essential for sustaining their value and building a legacy of health. By tracking metrics, refining strategies, and sharing success stories, organisations can create a wellness culture that endures.

Action Step Recap:

1. Define clear KPIs and implement tools to track wellness metrics.
2. Use data to identify gaps, test new initiatives, and refine existing programs.
3. Build a legacy of health by documenting best practices and communicating impact externally.

A commitment to measurement isn't just about accountability—it's about ensuring that your wellness initiatives remain impactful, relevant, and inspiring for years to come.

This chapter provides a comprehensive guide to measuring and refining wellness programs, helping organisations demonstrate their value and build sustainable, health-focused cultures.

CHAPTER 11

Lifelong Learning and Wellness – Fostering Continuous Growth

Introduction: The Intersection of Learning and Wellness

In a rapidly evolving world, the ability to learn and adapt is essential for both individuals and organisations. Lifelong learning—the commitment to ongoing personal and professional development—supports not only career growth but also overall well-being. A workplace that integrates learning and wellness creates an environment where employees can thrive holistically, balancing skill development with physical, mental, and emotional health.

This chapter explores how organisations can foster a culture of continuous growth, integrating learning opportunities into wellness programs and creating a workforce that is adaptable, resilient, and engaged.

Why Lifelong Learning is Essential for Wellness

1. Mental Stimulation and Cognitive Health

- Continuous learning keeps the mind sharp, reducing cognitive decline and promoting mental well-being.
- Employees who engage in learning report higher levels of focus, creativity, and problem-solving abilities.

2. Emotional Resilience

- Learning builds confidence and adaptability, helping employees navigate challenges with greater ease.
- Acquiring new skills fosters a sense of achievement and purpose, reducing stress and burnout.

3. Organisational Success

- A workforce committed to growth is more innovative, collaborative, and prepared for change.
- Integrating learning into wellness programs ensures employees are equipped to meet both personal and professional goals.

Building a Culture of Lifelong Learning

1. Promote a Growth Mindset

- **What It Is**: Encouraging employees to view challenges as opportunities for growth and development.
- **Action Steps**:
    - Provide training for managers on fostering a growth mindset within their teams.
    - Celebrate learning efforts, not just outcomes, to encourage experimentation and persistence.
    - Share stories of employees who successfully developed new skills or overcame obstacles through learning.

2. Integrate Learning into Wellness Programs

- **What It Is**: Combining wellness initiatives with skill development opportunities to address the whole person.
- **Action Steps**:
    - Offer workshops that blend wellness and learning, such as stress management, leadership training, or time management.
    - Create multidisciplinary programs that focus on both career growth and personal health.
    - Use gamification to make learning and wellness activities engaging and rewarding.

3. Create Personalised Learning Pathways

- **What It Is**: Tailoring development opportunities to individual employees' goals and needs.
- **Action Steps**:
    - Use surveys or assessments to understand employees' learning preferences and career aspirations.
    - Offer flexible learning options, such as online courses, mentorship programs, or certifications.
    - Provide regular feedback and coaching to help employees stay on track.

Leveraging Technology for Lifelong Learning

1. AI-Driven Learning Platforms

- **What They Are**: Personalised platforms that recommend learning resources based on employee goals and performance.
- **Action Steps**:
    - Partner with vendors to implement AI-powered learning management systems.
    - Use data to track employee progress and identify skill gaps.
    - Encourage employees to set learning goals and use the platform to achieve them.

2. Microlearning Modules

- **What They Are**: Bite-sized learning opportunities that fit into employees' busy schedules.
- **Action Steps**:
    - Develop short, engaging content on topics like mindfulness, communication skills, or leadership.

Chapter 11

- Integrate microlearning into existing tools, such as intranet portals or wellness apps.
- Offer incentives for completing modules, such as wellness points or certifications.

3. Virtual and Augmented Reality

- **What They Are**: Immersive learning experiences that simulate real-world scenarios.
- **Action Steps**:
    - Use VR for wellness-related training, such as guided meditations or virtual fitness classes.
    - Develop AR applications that provide interactive learning experiences, such as role-playing leadership scenarios.

Encouraging Peer Learning and Collaboration

1. Mentorship Programs

- **What They Are**: Pairing employees with mentors who can guide their development and share valuable insights.
- **Action Steps**:
    - Match mentors and mentees based on goals, interests, and experiences.
    - Provide training for mentors to ensure they are equipped to offer effective support.
    - Regularly check in to evaluate the success of mentorship relationships.

2. Knowledge Sharing Platforms

- **What They Are**: Digital or in-person forums where employees can share expertise and learn from one another.
- **Action Steps**:

- Create online communities where employees can discuss topics, ask questions, and share resources.
- Host knowledge-sharing events, such as lunch-and-learns or panel discussions.
- Encourage employees to contribute content, such as articles or videos, to the platform.

3. Team-Based Learning Activities

- **What They Are**: Collaborative learning experiences that build skills while strengthening social connections.
- **Action Steps**:
  - Organise team-building exercises focused on problem-solving, creativity, or innovation.
  - Use escape rooms, hackathons, or group challenges to make learning fun and interactive.
  - Provide opportunities for teams to present their learnings and share ideas with the organisation.

Real-World Example: Microsoft's Growth-Focused Culture

Microsoft has successfully integrated lifelong learning into its corporate culture through initiatives like:

1. **Growth Mindset Training**: All employees are trained to embrace a growth mindset, focusing on continuous improvement and adaptability.
2. **LinkedIn Learning**: Employees have access to an extensive library of courses on topics ranging from technical skills to personal development.
3. **Hackathons**: Annual events encourage employees to collaborate on innovative projects, fostering creativity and skill development.

These efforts have enhanced employee engagement and positioned Microsoft as a leader in innovation and adaptability.

Chapter 11

Measuring the Impact of Lifelong Learning Programs

1. Participation Metrics

- Track how many employees are engaging with learning opportunities, such as courses, workshops, or mentorship programs.

2. Learning Outcomes

- Assess changes in skills, knowledge, or performance as a result of learning initiatives.

3. Wellness Metrics

- Measure the impact of learning on employees' mental and emotional well-being, such as reduced stress or increased job satisfaction.

4. Organisational Metrics

- Analyse the broader impact of learning programs on business performance, such as productivity, innovation, or retention rates.

Actionable Step: Launch a Lifelong Learning Initiative

Here's how to get started:

1. **Assess Needs**: Survey employees to identify their learning preferences, goals, and challenges.

2. **Design Programs**: Develop a mix of learning opportunities, from workshops to online courses, that align with both individual and organisational goals.

3. **Promote Engagement**: Use internal communications, incentives, and leadership support to encourage participation.

4. **Measure Success**: Track participation, learning outcomes, and well-being metrics to refine your approach over time.

Conclusion: Learning as a Path to Wellness and Growth

Lifelong learning is more than a career tool—it's a wellness strategy that supports mental, emotional, and professional growth. By fostering a culture of continuous development, organisations can empower employees to thrive while building a resilient, future-ready workforce.

Action Step Recap:

1. Promote a growth mindset and integrate learning into wellness programs.

2. Use technology to deliver personalised, accessible, and engaging learning opportunities.

3. Encourage peer learning and collaboration through mentorship and team-based activities.

A workplace that values learning, and wellness creates a foundation for enduring success, helping employees and organisations grow together.

This chapter highlights the integration of lifelong learning and wellness, offering actionable strategies to foster continuous growth.

CHAPTER 12

Global Perspectives and Future Trends in Corporate Wellness

Introduction: Learning from the World

Corporate wellness is not a one-size-fits-all concept—it evolves based on cultural values, societal norms, and emerging technologies. By drawing inspiration from global practices and anticipating future trends, organisations can design wellness programs that are both innovative and inclusive.

In this final chapter, we'll explore global perspectives on wellness, showcasing cultural practices that can inspire holistic well-being. We'll also dive into future trends, such as biofeedback technology, environmental wellness, and the increasing role of AI, to help organisations prepare for what's next in corporate wellness.

Global Wellness Practices to Inspire Your Organisation

1. Japan: The Concept of Ikigai

- **What It Is**: Ikigai translates to "reason for being" and emphasises aligning work with personal purpose and passion.
- **How It Applies to Wellness**:
    - Encourage employees to identify what they love, what they're good at, and how it contributes to their organisation's mission.
    - Offer career coaching and mentorship programs that align personal goals with professional growth.
- **Action Steps**:
    - Host workshops where employees explore their Ikigai.

- Integrate purpose-driven goal setting into performance reviews.

2. Sweden: The Lagom Principle

- **What It Is**: Lagom means "just the right amount" and promotes balance and moderation in all aspects of life.
- **How It Applies to Wellness**:
    - Create work environments that discourage overwork and prioritise work-life balance.
    - Encourage "fika" breaks—short social breaks to relax and recharge.
- **Action Steps**:
    - Implement flexible work policies that allow for personal time and balance.
    - Design office spaces with relaxation areas for informal gatherings and breaks.

3. Brazil: The Power of Community (Jeitinho Brasileiro)

- **What It Is**: Jeitinho Brasileiro, or the "Brasilian way," reflects a culture of creativity, adaptability, and strong social bonds.
- **How It Applies to Wellness**:
    - Foster a sense of community through team-building activities and social wellness programs.
    - Encourage creative problem-solving and collaboration in the workplace.
- **Action Steps**:
    - Host regular community-driven events, such as group volunteering or cultural celebrations.
    - Create peer mentorship programs to strengthen interpersonal connections.

4. India: The Practice of Yoga and Mindfulness

- **What It Is**: Ancient practices like yoga and mindfulness are central to holistic wellness in Indian culture.
- **How It Applies to Wellness**:
  - Incorporate mindfulness and yoga sessions into wellness programs.
  - Promote practices that reduce stress and enhance focus.
- **Action Steps**:
  - Offer weekly yoga or meditation classes for employees.
  - Provide access to mindfulness apps and resources.

5. South Korea: The Value of Community Care

- **What It Is**: South Korea emphasises collectivism and mutual support, with a focus on community well-being.
- **How It Applies to Wellness**:
  - Encourage team-based wellness initiatives that build camaraderie and mutual accountability.
  - Promote a culture of caring, where employees support one another's well-being.
- **Action Steps**:
  - Create team-based challenges, such as group fitness goals or charity drives.
  - Train managers to foster supportive environments where employees feel cared for.

Future Trends in Corporate Wellness

1. Biofeedback and Wearable Technology

- **What It Is**: Devices that measure physiological responses, such as heart rate, stress levels, and sleep quality, to provide real-time wellness insights.
- **Applications**:
    - Use biofeedback tools to help employees manage stress through guided breathing or meditation.
    - Track collective wellness metrics to identify organisational trends and needs.
- **Action Steps**:
    - Offer wearable devices as part of wellness programs.
    - Partner with vendors to provide data-driven insights and personalised wellness plans.

2. Environmental Wellness

- **What It Is**: A focus on creating healthier, more sustainable workplaces that support physical and mental well-being.
- **Applications**:
    - Design offices with biophilic elements, such as natural light, plants, and improved air quality.
    - Encourage eco-friendly commuting options and sustainability practices.
- **Action Steps**:
    - Conduct an environmental wellness audit of your workplace.
    - Launch green initiatives, such as carpooling programs or zero-waste challenges.

3. Artificial Intelligence (AI) in Wellness

- **What It Is**: AI-powered platforms that deliver personalised wellness resources and insights based on employee data.

- **Applications**:
    - Use AI to recommend tailored wellness programs, such as fitness routines or mental health resources.
    - Leverage chatbots for real-time wellness support and emotional check-ins.

- **Action Steps**:
    - Implement AI-driven wellness platforms that adapt to individual needs.
    - Ensure transparency about how data is collected and used to maintain employee trust.

4. Mental Health and Neurodiversity

- **What It Is**: Increased emphasis on supporting mental health and creating inclusive workplaces for neurodiverse employees.

- **Applications**:
    - Provide tailored resources for mental health, such as therapy sessions or resilience training.
    - Offer accommodations for neurodiverse employees, such as sensory-friendly workspaces.

- **Action Steps**:
    - Develop mental health first aid training for managers and leaders.
    - Create resource groups or workshops focused on supporting neurodiversity.

5. Hybrid Work and Digital Wellness

- **What It Is**: Balancing the demands of remote and in-office work with wellness initiatives that support employees in both settings.

- **Applications**:
  - Offer remote-friendly wellness programs, such as virtual fitness classes and telehealth options.
  - Set boundaries around digital communication to prevent burnout.

- **Action Steps**:
  - Create a hybrid wellness strategy that addresses the unique needs of remote workers.
  - Use virtual tools to connect employees and build a sense of community.

Actionable Step: Create a Global Wellness Think Tank

To integrate global practices and prepare for future trends, establish a **Global Wellness Think Tank**:

1. **Gather Insights**: Form a diverse team of employees, leaders, and external experts to explore international wellness practices and trends.
2. **Experiment and Pilot**: Test new ideas in small groups before rolling them out across the organisation.
3. **Evaluate and Scale**: Use feedback and data to refine initiatives and scale successful programs.

Real-World Example: Google's Global Wellness Approach

Google's wellness initiatives reflect a blend of global practices and future-focused trends:

- **Mindfulness Programs**: Inspired by Eastern traditions, Google offers mindfulness and meditation sessions to enhance focus and reduce stress.

- **Hybrid Work Solutions**: Google's wellness programs include virtual fitness classes, mental health support, and ergonomic resources for remote workers.

- **Sustainability Initiatives**: The company integrates environmental wellness through green office designs and eco-friendly commuting options.

These efforts demonstrate how global perspectives, and future trends can create a holistic and innovative wellness strategy.

Conclusion: Preparing for the Future of Wellness

The future of corporate wellness lies in embracing diversity, leveraging technology, and staying ahead of emerging trends. By integrating global practices and preparing for what's next, organisations can create wellness programs that are adaptable, inclusive, and impactful.

Action Step Recap:

1. Explore global wellness practices and integrate relevant ideas into your programs.

2. Stay informed about future trends, such as biofeedback, environmental wellness, and AI-driven platforms.

3. Create a Global Wellness Think Tank to continuously innovate and refine your approach.

A forward-thinking, globally inspired wellness strategy ensures your organisation remains resilient, adaptable, and aligned with the needs of a diverse and evolving workforce.

This final chapter ties together global insights and future trends, positioning organisations to lead the way in corporate wellness.

CONCLUSION

Achieving Lasting Corporate Wellness – A Regenerative Vision for the Future

Introduction: The Journey to a Regenerative Workplace

Corporate wellness is no longer a "nice-to-have" initiative—it is a critical strategy for building resilient, sustainable, and thriving organisations. As we've explored throughout this book, the regenerative approach goes beyond maintaining the status quo; it's about creating environments where individuals and organisations flourish together, adapting to challenges while building a foundation for enduring success.

This concluding chapter reflects on the key principles and actions shared throughout the book, providing a cohesive vision for leaders to implement a regenerative wellness culture. It is a call to action for organisations to prioritise wellness as a fundamental driver of innovation, resilience, and long-term impact.

The Regenerative Workplace: A Transformative Vision

The regenerative workplace is built on three guiding principles:

1. Holistic Wellness

- Wellness must address all dimensions of human well-being—physical, mental, emotional, financial, social, and environmental.
- Programs should be inclusive, adaptable, and aligned with diverse employee needs.

2. Continuous Growth

- Organisations thrive when their people thrive. Prioritising learning, innovation, and adaptability ensures the workforce is prepared for future challenges.

Conclusion

- Wellness is a journey, not a destination. It requires constant refinement based on feedback and changing circumstances.

3. Long-Term Sustainability

- Wellness must be integrated into organisational strategies to create lasting impact. This includes aligning wellness with sustainability, resilience, and corporate responsibility goals.

Key Lessons from the Regenerative Wellness Framework

1. Leadership is the Foundation

- Leaders must champion wellness by modelling behaviours, fostering a supportive culture, and aligning wellness initiatives with organisational goals.
- Empathy, resilience, and purpose-driven leadership are essential for inspiring teams.

2. Personalisation Drives Engagement

- One-size-fits-all approaches fail to address the diverse needs of today's workforce. Tailored wellness programs that reflect generational, cultural, and individual differences drive participation and impact.

3. Data is a Powerful Tool

- Measuring the effectiveness of wellness initiatives ensures accountability and continuous improvement. Use data to align programs with employee needs and organisational objectives.

4. Technology and Innovation Enable Progress

- Embrace wearable devices, AI-driven platforms, and other technological advancements to enhance personalisation, accessibility, and effectiveness in wellness programs.

5. Global Perspectives Enhance Impact

- Drawing inspiration from global wellness practices fosters innovation and inclusivity, while preparing organisations to address future trends.

Building a Five-Year Wellness Roadmap

To make corporate wellness a long-term priority, organisations should develop a comprehensive roadmap. Here's how to create one:

Year 1: Laying the Foundation

- Conduct a wellness audit to assess current strengths and gaps.
- Train leaders to champion wellness and build resilience within their teams.
- Launch pilot programs focused on key wellness dimensions, such as mental health or financial wellness.

Year 2-3: Scaling and Integrating

- Expand successful programs to reach more employees.
- Integrate wellness metrics into organisational KPIs and performance reviews.
- Align wellness initiatives with broader goals, such as sustainability or community engagement.

Year 4: Innovating and Refining

- Introduce cutting-edge technologies, such as AI or biofeedback devices, to enhance personalisation and engagement.
- Explore global wellness practices to diversify and enrich programs.
- Use employee feedback and data to refine and adapt initiatives.

Conclusion

Year 5: Building a Legacy

- Publish a wellness impact report to showcase progress and inspire continued commitment.
- Develop a mentorship program to pass on wellness leadership skills.
- Celebrate milestones and recognise wellness champions within the organisation.

The Transformational Impact of Wellness

By embracing a regenerative approach to wellness, organisations can achieve:

1. **Enhanced Employee Engagement**: Employees who feel supported are more productive, innovative, and committed.
2. **Resilience Against Challenges**: A wellness-first culture equips organisations to navigate crises and disruptions with confidence.
3. **A Strong Employer Brand**: Companies known for prioritising wellness attract top talent and build lasting reputations.
4. **Sustainable Growth**: Integrating wellness with corporate strategies drives long-term success for employees, organisations, and communities.

Call to Action: Become a Wellness Pioneer

This book is not just a guide—it's a call to action for leaders to create a workplace that reflects their values, supports their people, and shapes a better future. To get started:

1. Commit to wellness as a core organisational value.
2. Take immediate action by implementing one initiative—whether it's a wellness audit, leadership training, or a new program.
3. Inspire others by sharing your wellness journey, encouraging a ripple effect of positive change.

Closing Words: A Legacy of Health and Purpose

As leaders, we have the power to create workplaces that don't just survive but thrive—places where people find purpose, resilience, and joy. By adopting a regenerative approach to wellness, you're not only investing in the well-being of your employees but also shaping the future of work itself.

The regenerative workplace is a vision for what's possible when we prioritise health, innovation, and sustainability. Together, we can build organisations that stand the test of time, making a lasting impact on employees, communities, and the world.

Thank you for taking this journey toward lasting corporate wellness. The work begins now—one step, one person, and one organisation at a time.

www.ingramcontent.com/pod-product-compliance
Lightning Source LLC
Chambersburg PA
CBHW020450220526
45464CB00002B/930